US AIR POWER

Modern Attack Planes

A member of the ground crew cleans the canopy of an A-10 Thunderbolt II, April 5, 1999, an A-10 assigned to the 81st Fighter Squadron deployed to Aviano Air Base, Italy in support of NATO Operation 'Allied Force'. The mighty A-10, nicknamed the 'Warthog', is renowned for its destructive power in the close support role.

US AIR POWER

Modern Attack Planes

Aircraft, Weapons and their Battlefield Might

Anthony A. Evans

Greenhill Books
LONDON

Stackpole Books
PENNSYLVANIA

Greenhill Books

Modern Attack Planes: Aircraft, Weapons and their Battlefield Might
first published 2004 by Greenhill Books,
Lionel Leventhal Limited, Park House, 1 Russell Gardens,
London NW11 9NN
www.greenhillbooks.com
and
Stackpole Books, 5067 Ritter Road, Mechanicsburg,
PA 17055, USA

British Library Cataloguing in Publication Data

Evans, Anthony A.
Modern attack planes: – (US air power: the illustrated
history of American air power, the campaigns, the
aircraft and the men)
1. United States. Air Force – Equipment and supplies
2. Air power – United States
3. Fighter planes – United States
4. United States – History, Military – 20th century
I. Titles
358.4'00973'09049

ISBN 1-85367-592-X

*Library of Congress Cataloging-in-Publication Data
available*
The photographs in this book are courtesy of the United
States Department of Defense, the United States Air
Force, the United States Navy and the United States
Marine Corps.

Designed by DAG Publications Ltd
Design by David Gibbons
Layout by Anthony A. Evans
Edited by Hugh Schoenemann
Printed in Singapore

US AIR POWER
MODERN ATTACK PLANES

The attack plane occupies the position set between a fighter and a bomber. Some are dedicated attack planes, others have a multi-role capability. Attack aircraft have to be able to attack both land and sea surface targets and have the ability to defend themselves while doing so, with the aid of Electronic Counter Measures (ECM), decoy systems and air-to-air missiles. The F-14, F-15, F-16 and F-18 fighters all have a multi-role capability which includes attack. The AV-8B Harrier II, A-10 Thunderbolt II and F-117 'stealthy' Nighthawk are primarily attack planes with other secondary roles. All can wield a very large assortment of conventional bombs, rockets, guided missiles and precision weapons, which make them indispensable on the modern battlefield.

Spring 2003 again demonstrated the successful use of modern attack planes in the skies over Iraq. The Iraqi army, and the much vaunted Republican Guard, simply folded under the punishing aerial assault dished out by US aircraft. With a combination of smart bombs, dumb bombs and guided missiles, they dominated the battlefield from the very first moments of the conflict. Twelve years earlier, during Desert Storm, TV viewers across the world watched as precision guided munitions (PGMs) destroyed bridges, buildings, parked aircraft, and a host of other military targets, with what seemed unerring accuracy and ease. The Iraqi armed forces simply crumpled under the weight of US air power, particularly her attack planes.

During the last twelve months of World War II it took over 100 B-17 bombers, dropping 600 bombs, to eliminate a point target (e.g. a bridge). During the Vietnam War it took 175 bombs to destroy a similar target. Today it only takes one precision guided bomb.

Today's attack planes are the direct descendants of the aircraft that fought in the skies over Vietnam some 30 or more years ago, such as the ubiquitous Phantom, the mighty Thunderchief, and prop-driven, WW2 vintage, Skyraider. The lessons learnt during that conflict were many and varied and were incorporated into today's descendants.

The tactics employed during war stress the importance of US aircraft quickly establishing dominance over the foe and her high-profile targets. The destruction of Command, Control and Communications (C3 systems) comes high on the target list. One of the first objectives is the destruction and suppression of enemy air-defense systems, blinding their early-warning capability and attacking their operating centers. Once the air defense systems have been knocked-out or disabled then the degradation of their air defense weapons begins – surface-to-air missiles (SAMs) and anti-aircraft artillery (AAA) – plus direct attacks on their air force, with round the clock raids on airfields and their aircraft.

The next phase is the destruction of strategic military and economic targets. Power plants, oil refineries, weapons production and storage facilities would be typical. Air interdiction would also destroy physical communications within the enemy's territory such as roads, railways, and bridges.

The following phase would be to prepare the way for any planned ground offensive. The enemy ground forces would first be isolated from their sources of supply and reinforcement then subjected to a relentless aerial bombardment. As General Colin Powell said about the Iraqi Army during the Gulf War of 1991: 'First we are going to cut it off, then we are going to kill it.' The destruction of tanks, artillery, and armored personnel carriers would be given a particularly high priority.

Next would come the phase in direct support of any ground offensive. Control of the air over one's army is vital. During any ground battle US troops are able to call in air assets as needed, for direct close air support in pursuance of their needs on the battlefield, such as attacking either stubborn defensive resistance or advancing enemy armoured columns.

Vietnam saw the first US use of precision guided munitions which have come to dominate today's battlefield. Vietnam also saw the development of the 'Wild Weasel', an aircraft type dedicated to the defense suppression mission. They carried special sensors to detect hostile air defense radars and counter the SAM threat, with on-board anti-radiation missiles that were then used to attack them.

The Suppression of Enemy Air Defenses (SEAD) is one of the most vital of missions in modern warfare. Hostile radars can be neutralised by electronic warfare aircraft, but SEAD warplanes endeavor to destroy them and the enemy defenses' SAMs. This is called a 'hard kill'. A 'soft kill' is when it may be sufficient to intimidate enemy radar sites into shutting down temporarily because of the threat of detection and subsequent attack with missiles such as the AGM-88 HARM (High-speed Anti-Radiation Missile). Dedicated SEAD aircraft may be used to suppress enemy SAM radar with a 'hard' or a 'soft kill', as did the 'Wild Weasels' during the Vietnam War.

During the war in Vietnam the concept for the A-10 Thunderbolt II (nicknamed 'Warthog') was conceived as a close support aircraft and a tank hunter. It was realised that supersonic fighters were less suitable for close support roles. What was needed was an aircraft that could lift a heavy and varied ordnance package as well as loiter for extended periods of time, and be able to survive fairly heavy battle damage. The A-10 has proved that it is well able to meet these criteria and has done so more than once, over the deserts of Iraq and the hills and mountains of the Balkans.

Free-fall bombs (known as 'iron' or 'dumb' bombs) seem out of place in the modern world of Global Positioning Satellites (GPS) and laser-guided technology. But they are cheap, straightforward, and easy to manufacture, so still play a prominent part in the attack plane's arsenal. A wide variety of these bombs, centred around the Mark 82 series and M117 weapons, can be fitted with a range of fuses and tails and form the basis of the US general purpose bomb arsenal. They include the cruciform flip-out air brake's tail called the 'Snake-eye' and the 'ballute' system of inflatable air brakes which slows the bomb down, allowing the attack plane to escape the blast and the debris.

The 'Interdicter' employs speed and sophisticated defenses to penetrate heavily defended areas and attack high value targets such as airfields, powerstations, etc. By virtue of their very nature, such targets are situated some way behind the front line and the aircraft therefore would have to fly over many miles of enemy held territory and the air defenses held therein.

During World War II, the torpedo bomber brought about the demise of a great many surface ships, both combat and merchant. The aircraft type has long since disappeared from the inventory of airforces worldwide as the aerial torpedo was replaced by air-launched anti-ship missile. The Harpoon missile, as used by the US, can be launched at great distances and home in on the target without even having to physically see the ship against which it is being fired.

Operation 'Prairie Fire'

With the political tension between the USA and Libya's dictator, Gaddafi, on March 24, 1986, several Libyan SA-5 surface-to-air missiles were launched against US Navy F-14 Tomcats that were patrolling the Gulf of Sirte in the Mediterranean. Fortunately no aircraft were hit. The US Navy retaliated by attacking three Libyan fast missile boats that were aggressively approaching the US Navy Battle Group from which the Tomcats had flown. The first was disabled by an AGM-84 Harpoon anti-ship missile and then blasted by Rockeye cluster bombs. Shortly after that another missile boat was hit and set on fire by a Harpoon. More Libyan SAMs were fired, but several of their radars were attacked with HARM missiles, disabling several of them. Next day another missile boat was intercepted by an A-6 and disabled with a Rockeye cluster bomb, then sunk using a Harpoon. There were no losses to the US Navy.

Operation 'El Dorado Canyon'

When, on April 2, 1986, Libyan terrorist agents set off a bomb in a Berlin discotheque frequented by GIs, the US decided to retaliate with aircraft flying from the carriers USS *America* and USS *Coral Sea* as well as USAF F-111s flying from the UK. First, USN F/A-18As armed with HARM anti-radiation missiles attacked SAM sites, before Libyan barracks and airbases were successfully blasted with a combination of 'dumb' bombs and laser-guided weapons. The results were at least two dozen Libyan aircraft destroyed or severely damaged along with the destruction of barracks and attacks made on other military sites. Unfortunately one F-111F was shot down.

'Desert Storm' and Iraq

The US-led coalition during the Gulf War of 1991 had certain priorities that guided its military operations during 'Desert Storm'. The first was to destroy the Iraqi leadership and C3 network. The second was to ground the Iraqi air force and destroy it. The third, to grind down the army and Saddam's Republican Guard before the land attack began. These priorities were to be carried out in an air campaign designed to take some 40 days.

On January 17, 1991, a F-117 stealth attack plane dropped the first bomb of the conflict on an air defense control center in Baghdad. US attack planes then proceeded to attack Iraqi airfields, communication centers, and other high-value targets as well as attacking military targets inside Kuwait. Then a sustained campaign began on the bridges that formed part of the enemy supply routes. When Iraqi Scud missiles then began to land on Israel and local coalition countries, a certain proportion of the allies' aviation assets were allocated to 'The Great Scud Hunt'.

The Iraqi forces began to pump crude oil into the sea, causing a massive oil slick in the Persian Gulf, intending to hamper any Coalition naval operations, however small, and instigating an environmental disaster. In a precision attack, TF-111Fs of the 48th Tactical Fighter Wing successfully disabled the pumping stations involved, stemming the flow of oil.

When Iraqi troops advanced across the border into Saudi Arabia and seized the town of Khafji, AV-8B and A-10 attack planes were used very effectively to help repulse the thrust.

By January 30, aerial attacks began to concentrate on the élite Iraqi Republican Guard. By February 5 it was claimed that as many as a third of their tanks had been destroyed, many by US attack planes.

When the land campaign began on February 24, attack aircraft began to directly support troops in the land battle. The campaign was over by midnight on the 28th.

When the war ended Operations 'Northern Watch' and 'Southern Watch' were initiated to impose No-Fly Zones on the Iraqi Air Force. The Iraqis moved up SAM and AAA batteries close to the zones. On January 13, 1993, a large strike force of US and coalition aircraft struck seventeen targets including Iraqi AAA, SAM and air defense command control sites.

More attacks were to follow over the years. The largest was on December 16, 1998. Operation 'Desert Fox' was launched to coincide with an attempted coup against Saddam Hussein by elements of the Iraqi Army. The four-day offensive introduced new weapons and tactics. During the first 24 hours of the campaign, attacks were conducted across Iraq, initially only by US Navy aircraft and cruise missiles, before then being joined by US Air Force planes as well as those of the British Royal Air Force. In all, the operation involved some 656 sorties as well as the use of more than 200 cruise missiles. About 100 targets were struck including ones against the Iraqi leadership, Republican Guard units and Iraq's possible development of weapons of mass destruction and the missiles to deliver them. The coup was sadly unsuccessful. Encounters between US aircraft and Iraqi forces continued to be ongoing, if sporadic.

The Balkans

US and other NATO nations first became involved in the former Yugoslavia in the summer of 1992 with Operation 'Deny Flight'. This was instigated in order to impose a UN No-Fly Zone to stop the warring factions there using their military aircraft against one another. NATO air strikes were also made on Serbian troops and AAA sites, and on the Serbian-held Udbina airbase in Croatia on November 21, 1994. In July 1995, Operation 'Deliberate Force' would see US and NATO carry out a widespread air offensive against the Bosnian Serbs' forces whenever they attacked designated 'safe areas'. On August 30, 1995, NATO's 5th Allied Tactical Air Force aircraft began a concentrated two week offensive triggered by a Serbian mortar attack on civilians in Sarajevo. Key Bosnian Serb air defense sites, SAM and artillery batteries, ammunition depots, command posts, communications towers, bridges, etc, came under US and NATO air attack. Some 708 precision guided munitions (PGMs) and 300 'iron' bombs were used during the air offensive. The Bosnian Serbs gave in to UN demands, allowing free access to Sarajevo and withdrew the artillery threatening the city. After signing the Dayton Peace Accords on December 20, 1995, Serbian, Croat and Bosnian political leaders ended the war, but NATO warplanes continued to patrol the skies.

Again, US and other NATO air forces were called on to go to war in the skies over the former Yugoslavia. This time it was because of the unresolved political and military deadlock over the land of Kosovo, whose people demanded independence from the Serbian/Yugoslavian State. The Serbian army of occupation was endulging in ethnic cleansing and committing attrocities against the Kosovan civilian population during the course of its guerrilla war with the local freedom fighters. The NATO air campaign acted on the evening of March 24, 1999, when the Serbian army refused to leave the country. Some 200 allied aircraft of the 5th Allied Tactical Air Force based in Italy would take part. They would be supported by ship and submarine-launched cruise missiles and American strategic bombers operating from bases in the UK and the USA.

US and allied strike aircraft hit more than twenty air defense sites around the Yugoslav capital of Belgrade as well as sites in Kosovo and Montenegro. The Suppression of Enemy Air Defenses was principally conducted by USAF F-16CJs, and USN and USMC EA-6B Electronic Warfare Prowlers. The pattern of strikes continued for nearly three weeks as the Serbian air defenses were systematically ground down, even though the Serbs did manage to bring down a USAF F-117 Nighthawk 'stealth' fighter near Belgrade.

Strategic targets were next earmarked for attack as Serbian atrocities and ethnic cleansing of the population of Kosovo intensified. Strike aircraft employed some 8,000 precision guided munitions during the 79 days of the air campaign. Serbian powerstations were hit, petroleum refining was completely knocked out, ammunition and military vehicle production severely hit, command and control badly disrupted, and 70% of bridges over the Danube destroyed. The country's infrastructure was coming apart.

Attack planes also roamed the skies over Kosovo, searching out and trying to hit Serbian armored vehicles, artillery, troops, supply dumps, and command posts, etc., which were often hidden in the center of villages. Tight rules of engagement had to be observed in order to prevent civilian casualties. Even so, by June 20 the Serbians' forces had to give up and their troops withdrew from Kosovo. Operation 'Allied Force' was at an end.

Operation 'Enduring Freedom'
The war against terrorism in Afghanistan began on October 7, 2001. Initially the US targeted the Taliban's somewhat limited Air Force, early warning radars, SAM sites, and command and control centers. Tomahawk cruise missiles, strategic bombers, and US Navy F/A-18 and F-14 planes were used during these strikes. The Navy attack planes were flying from the carriers USS *Carl Vinson* and *Enterprise,* operating in the Indian Ocean. The planes used the whole gamut of precision weapons available to them. When US ground forces had moved in and established themselves, USAF and Air National Guard attack planes arrived in the operational theater to provide support to them. The back of the Taliban was broken and by the end of November/early December negotiations for the surrender of Taliban military forces were underway. But Osama bin Laden and his Al-Qaeda fighters remain elusive. The air strikes continue in support of the international forces that are based there in the ongoing fight against terrorists.

Operation 'Iraqi Freedom'
March 19, 2003 saw US attack planes again at the forefront during the invasion of Iraq. A highly successful month-long air campaign was conducted by US aircraft along with those of the British and Australian Air Forces. Over 41,000 sorties were flown, more than half being ground-support missions, dropping or firing nearly 30,000 munitions. Of these, over 20,000 were guided and the remainder were 'dumb' weapons ranging from 750lb M117 bombs to 2,000lb Mk 84s and cluster bombs. After a campaign lasting some 720 hours, the only attack plane to be lost to enemy action was an A-10, even though many others suffered damage of various kinds. US war planes are still supporting the occupation force.

A US Air Force A-10A 'Warthog' from the 52nd Fighter Wing, 81st Fighter Squadron, Spangdahlem Air Base, Germany, in flight during a NATO Operation 'Allied Force' combat mission. The 52nd Fighter Wing A-10As deployed to Aviano Air Base, Italy, are specially designed for close air support of ground forces. The A-10 'Tank Killer' munitions include bombs, electronic jamming pods, 2.75 inch 'Zuni' rockets pods, AGM-65D Maverick missiles, Sidewinder air-to-air missiles, and a massive 30mm cannon mounted in the nose.

Left: Once the mainstay of NATO's anti-tank forces, the A-10 would have opposed the massed tanks of the Warsaw Pact if the 'Cold War' had gone 'Hot'. The A-10 devastated Iraqi armor during Operation 'Desert Storm' in 1991, notching up huge kill tallies. The pilots were flying in a very rich target enviroment. In the former Yugoslavia the A-10 was seen in action rooting out hidden Serbian military positions.

Below and opposite page: Able to penetrate hostile airspace and attack vital enemy targets without being detected by radar defenses, the F-117 'Stealth' Nighthawk has seen action over the jungles of Panama in 1989, the deserts of Iraq, and the mountains of the Balkans. The F-117 uses its sophisticated target aquisition and designation abilities, scoring vital hits against targets with pinpoint accuracy. The renowned Lockheed 'Skunk Works' designed and developed the F-117 within a surprisingly low budget for such a sophisticated plane. A total of only 59 production aircraft have been delivered to the US Air Force, but the F-117 force is able to exert an influence on an air campaign that far outweighs the force's meagre size.

Above: The F-14 Tomcat is primarily an air superiority plane but, as early as 1972, a Tomcat flew with 18 Mk 82 500lb bombs, plus a complement of missiles. The first bombs were dropped from an in-service Navy Tomcat on August 8, 1990. With the retirement of the Intruder, the 'Bombcat', as it is nicknamed, is now widely used in air-to-ground missions, and has seen action in the Balkans, Afghanistan and Iraq.

Below: In the early 1980s the US Air Force had a requirement for a new multi-role fighter to supplement the F-111, and selected a two-seat development of the F-15, the F-15E. Many have seen combat in the Gulf Wars, as well as over the Balkans and Afghanistan. This is an F-15E 'Strike Eagle' from the 492nd Fighter Squadron, Royal Air Force Lakenheath, England, releasing a GBU-28 'Bunker Buster' laser-guided bomb. The GBU-28 was designed and first used during the Persian Gulf War in 1991 to destroy hardened targets such as bunkers and underground command centers.

Right: An F-16 Fighting Falcon dropping two Joint Direct Attack Munitions (JDAM) precision guided bombs. The F-16 can carry up to 12,000lb of ordnance including air-to-ground missiles, precision guided bombs, anti-radar missiles, anti-ship missiles, and rocket pods. It is one of the most versatile attack planes in US service.

Below: An F-16 with Rockeye cluster bombs hanging from outer wing pylons, with external fuel tanks on the inner pylons and an AN/ALQ-119(V)-17 Electronic Counter Measures (ECM) pod under the fuselage.

Left: An F/A-18C Hornet flying from carrier USS *Harry S. Truman* (CVN 75) on a combat mission over Iraq during Operation 'Iraqi Freedom' in the Spring of 2003. It is armed with two laser-guided bombs and one JDAM bomb plus two Sidewinders and an AMRAAM air-to-air missile. The F/A-18 is capable of carrying up to 15,500lbs of weaponry.

Below: Aviation ordnancemen assigned to the 'Ragin' Bulls' of Strike Fighter Squadron Three Seven (VFA-37) rig support suspension equipment to load a 2,000lb GBU-31 Joint Direct Attack Munitions (JDAM) onto the wing of an F/A-18 Hornet.

Munitions specialists preparing to load an AGM-65 Maverick air-to-surface missile onto an A-10 for a sortie during Operation 'Desert Storm' over Iraq. The Maverick is used by all three US air services, with over 5,300 being fired during Operation 'Desert Storm'. During the Vietnam War it was used in combat trials in 1972 and it officially entered squadron service in 1973. The missile has been upgraded over the years and is still one of the finest missiles of its type anywhere in the world.

Above: An air-to-air view of a US Marine Corps AV-8B Harrier II attack plane from Marine Attack Squadron Five One Three (VMA-513) during Operation 'Desert Storm' in early 1991.

Left: Aboard USS *Nassau* (LHA 4), April 14, 1999, a AV-8B Harrier II lands vertically following an attack mission into Kosovo. Part of the USS *Nassau*'s amphibious battle group, the Harriers have launched strikes in support of NATO Operation 'Allied Force'. The US Marine Corps is the largest operator in the world of the British-conceived 'jump jet'.

Above: An A-10A Thunderbolt II attack plane armed with two AIM-9 Sidewinders, two AGM-65 Maverick missiles and four Mk 82 500lb bombs. Note on the starbord wing the ALQ-119 electronic countermeasures pod and just visible hanging from the starbord side of the fuselage can be seen the Pave Pennylaser receiver and tracking pod.

Below: An A-10 fires its 30mm GAU-8/A Avenger seven-barrelled Gatling gun. It can fire 4,000 rounds per minute and is capable of defeating an array of different ground targets. The Thunderbolt II is an attack aircraft that was built expressly for close air support of ground forces, particularly as an anti-tank aircraft.

Opposite page: An OA-10 pilot from the 442nd Fighter Wing straps and buckles up for flight. The unit was deployed to Aviano Air Base in Italy in support of Operation 'Decisive Edge' in Bosnia in 1996. Although given a different designation the OA-10 and the A-10 are identical, but their missions differ. OA-10s are tasked with Forward Air Control (FAC) and target marking, providing a direct link between ground control officers and attack planes.

Above and below: The same OA-10 as seen on the opposite page is armed with two Maverick air-to-ground missiles, Sidewinder air-to-air missiles and two LAU-68 rocket pods. Each pod contains seven rockets which are used for target marking purposes.

Above: Munition specialists from the 23rd Tactical Fighter Wing loading 30mm rounds into an A-10's GAU-8/A Avenger cannon prior to a sortie. The gun and ammunition have a gross weight of some two tons, the ammunition drum containing 1,174 rounds.

Below: Although different types of ammunition are available, the most common mix carried by the aircraft is one High Explosive Incendiary (HEI) round for every five Armour Piercing Incendiary (API) rounds. The API round warhead is made of depleted (non-radioactive) uranium which is extremely dense; these 1.5lb milk-bottle-size 30mm cannon shells ripped through the tanks and armored vehicles of Saddam's army.

Above and below: 81st Fighter Squadron munitions specialists remove an AGM-65 Maverick Missile from its case, and then proceed to load it onto an A-10 Thunderbolt. The early versions of the Maverick used a small TV camera in the nose to see and lock onto its target. The more recent variants have either laser or infra-red guidance. Aviano Air Base, Italy, supporting NATO Operation 'Allied Force' over Kosovo in 1999.

Above and below: Loading a Maverick air-to-ground missile onto an A-10. The AGM-65 Maverick is the principal weapon and is used for stand-off precision attacks. Two types of seeker heads can be used: the imaging infra-red seeker and the TV scene magnification seeker. The missile is 8ft 2in (2.49m) long, with a wing span of 2ft 4in (0.72m). The infra-red version weighs in at 485lbs and the TV version at 463lbs, with either a shaped-charge warhead or a blast-fragmentation warhead. The A-10 pilot must climb to get a good view of the target. He then selects one of his Mavericks and uses the image supplied by the missile's seeker head, transmitted to a screen in his cockpit, to acquire and designate the target, with the aid of cross-hairs on the screen. On launch, the missile holds the target image in its own memory, guiding itself to impact as the A-10 attack plane escapes the area.

Above and below: A triple-pylon carrying three Maverick missiles. Also seen is an LAU-68 rocket pod and an ALQ-131 electronic countermeasures pod.

Above: An A-10 Thunderbolt from the 81st Fighter Squadron, being loaded with six AGM-65 Maverick missiles, six Mk 82 500lb bombs, two AIM-9 missiles, two LAU-68 rocket pods and an ALQ-131 electronic countermeasures pod, sits on the tarmac at Aviano Air Base, Italy, 1999.

Opposite page, top and bottom: These US Air Force A-10A 'Warthogs', from the 52nd Fighter Wing, 81st Fighter Squadron in flight during a NATO Operation 'Allied Force' combat mission. These A-10s each carry two Mk 82 500lb 'dumb' bombs, an ALQ-131 electronic jamming pod, two AGM-65D Mavericks, two LAU-68 rocket pods and two Sidewinder air-to-air missiles. Note Pave Pennylaser receiver and tracking pod under the forward starboard side of the fuselage.

Below: The pilot of an A-10 Thunderbolt from the 81st Fighter Squadron gives the thumbs-up sign before taxiing down the runway, Aviano Air Base, Italy, while supporting NATO Operation 'Allied Force' over Kosovo in 1999.

Above: This 'Warthog' stands in front of some Hardened Aircraft Shelters (HAS). The plane carries four LAU-68 rocket pods for target marking in its FAC role. The A-10 has a maximum weapon load of 16,000lbs of mixed ordnance on eleven external store stations.

Below: The A-10 has a combat radius of 620 miles on deep strike missions and 288 miles in its close support role with 1.7 hour loiter time. Its maximum speed is 439 mph and its maximum weight is 50,000lbs. Two General Electric TF34-GE-100 turbofans power the plane, each rated at 9,065lb of static thrust.

Above and below: A-10s operate in pairs and have the ability to sneak up on the enemy by utilizing terrain and flying very low. When attacking a target such as a convoy, the two A-10s will attack from different directions, one destroying the front vehicle and the other the rear vehicle in the column, thereby trapping it and impeding its escape. Each plane then flies a figure of eight pattern over the convoy, between them maintaining a continuous pattern of fire. Note in the lower photograph this A-10 is carrying two Rockeye cluster bombs on the innermost starboard stores pylon.

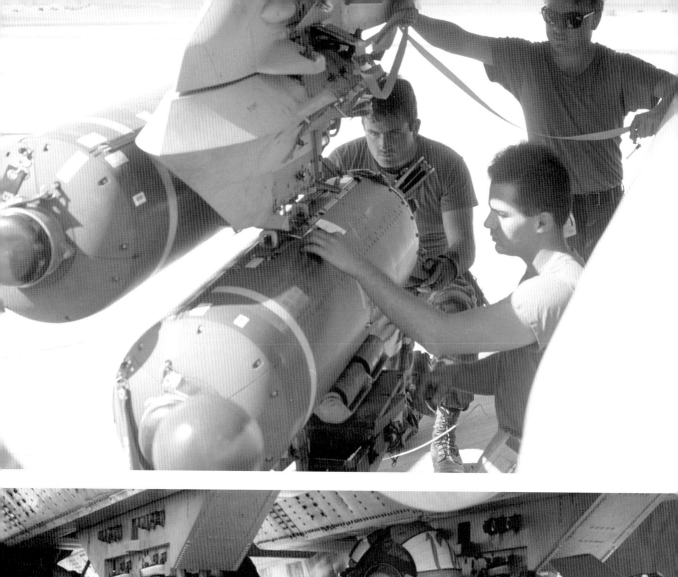

Opposite page top: Loading SUU-65 tactical munition dispensers (cluster bombs) onto an attack plane during Operation 'Desert Shield'. The SUU-65 contains 214 submunitions and the bomb features 'pop-up' tail surfaces which spin the weapon at 2,500rpm after release as it travels through the air, for an optimum spread of the submunitions as they are dispensed.

Above: A GBU-12 500lb laser-guided bomb on an F/A-18 Hornet as it prepares to be launched from the flight deck aboard the aircraft carrier USS *Kitty Hawk* (CV 63). *Kitty Hawk* and her embarked Carrier Air Wing Five (CVW-5) were operating with coalition forces in support of Operation 'Iraqi Freedom', the multi-national coalition effort to liberate the Iraqi people and end the regime of Saddam Hussein.

Left and below: JDAM GPS-guided bombs. In this case 2,000lb Mk 84 'dumb' bombs have been reconfigured by attaching a GPS guidance unit and fins which turn them into precision guided bombs.

Above: An F-117 Nighthawk pulls onto the tarmac after returning from a mission during Operation 'Iraqi Freedom' in the spring of 2003. This jet displays sixteen combat mission marks. During Operation 'Desert Storm', in 1991, an F-117 dropped the very first bomb of the war.

Left and right: With its extraordinary faceted shape and revolutionary radar defeating features, the F-117 'Stealth' fighters are able to penetrate hostile airspace without being seen by radars or infra-red sensors. The F-117 can then use its sophisticated guidance and targeting systems to score hits with pinpoint accuracy. A reduced radar cross-section is achieved by the sharp angular shape of the aircraft which scatters radar returns back in multiple directions.

Above: The primary weapon of the F-117A is the 2,000lb GBU-27A/B laser-guided bomb (LGB) fitted with the hardened BLU-109/B penetrator warhead. This weapon was used to great effect during 'Desert Storm' in 1991. The plane has an internal, slender bomb bay which contains two weapon-bearing hoists. The primary role of the F-117 is to attack high-value targets such as leadership and command bunkers, which is why the hardened penetrator warhead is needed by the GBU-27A/B. During 'Desert Storm' the F-117 destroyed 40% of all strategic targets, but flew only 2% of strike sorties.

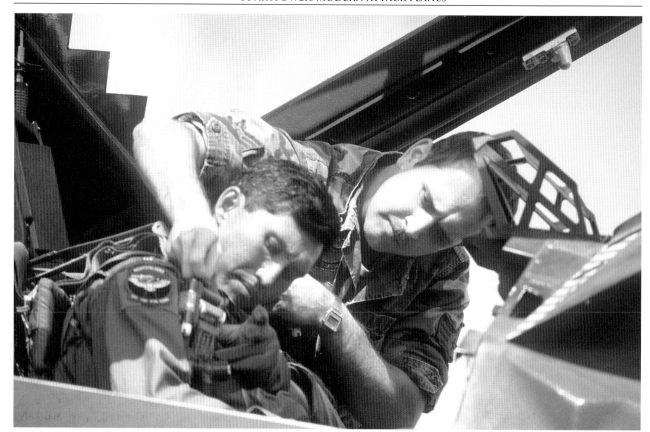

Opposite page, top and bottom: Many view the F-117 'Stealth' pilots as an élite within an élite, having accomplished many thousands of hours on more conventional fighter, bomber and attack planes. The pilots are chosen as much for their qualities of stable temperament as for their flying skills.

Above and below: The F-117 has a maximum weapons load of 5,000lb with a range of 535 miles at 30,000ft. Its maximum level speed is 646mph at optimum altitude and it is powered by two General Electric F404-GE-F1D2 non-afterburning turbofans each rated at 10,800lb maximum thrust. It carries no defensive armament, relying on its stealth capability to avoid enemy defenses.

Left: A 37th Tactical Fighter Wing F-117A stealth fighter refuels from a 22nd Air Refuelling Wing KC-10 Extender aircraft while en route to Saudi Arabia during Operation 'Desert Shield'.

Opposite page, top: The F-15E Strike Eagle has become the benchmark against which other attack planes are measured. The Strike Eagle was developed specifically to supplant the long-range F-111 strike bomber. Entering service in 1988, it has seen combat in all the major air campaigns since then.

Opposite page, bottom: An F-15E Strike Eagle drops four GBU-27 laser-guided bombs over the ranges north of Nellis Air Force Base, Nevada, during a training mission.

Below: Two reinforced hardened concrete aircraft hangars at the Ahmed Al Jaber Airfield in Iraq, showing the results of a coalition bombing strike during Operation 'Desert Storm'. The hits on the hangars would have destroyed any aircraft inside.

A KC-10A Extender refuels an F-15E Strike Eagle on a combat mission over Iraq during Operation 'Iraqi Freedom'. The aircraft is part of the 380th Air Expeditionary Wing at a forward-deployed location. The F-15E is from the 48th Fighter Wing and is equipped with GBU-12 Paveway II 500lb laser-guided bombs and LANTIRN navigational pods under the fuselage and AIM-120 AMRAAM and AIM-9 Sidewinder air-to-air missiles under the wings.

Above: Over northern Iraq, an F-14 Tomcat that was embarked aboard the aircraft carrier USS *Harry S. Truman* (CVN 75) flies a combat mission in direct support of Operation 'Iraqi Freedom'. The F-14 Tomcat is a twin-engine, variable-sweep-wing fighter whose primary missions are air superiority and fleet air defense as well as precision strikes. This F-14 is configured for attacking ground targets with laser-guided bombs, plus Sidewinder missiles for shooting down any enemy planes that it might apprehend.

Below: An F-14 Tomcat assigned to the 'Bounty Hunters' of Fighter Squadron Two (VF-2) displays the bomb symbols below the canopy indicating the number and type of mission that this Tomcat has carried out in support of Operation 'Iraqi Freedom'. Although it was not originally assigned a ground-attack mission, the F-14's under-fuselage pallets, which would ordinarily carry Phoenix missiles, can also mount bomb racks for 1,000lb Mk 83 or 2,000lb Mk 84 bombs, or other free-fall weaponry.

Sailors aboard the aircraft carrier USS *Constellation* (CV 64) perform routine maintenance on an F-14D Tomcat with a 2,000lb version of the JDAM, designated the GBU-32, in preparation for evening flight operations over the Southern Iraqi No-Fly Zone (NFZ). A JDAM can be launched from approximately fifteen miles from the target and each is independently targeted by GPS. The *Constellation* was deployed to the Arabian Gulf in support of Operations 'Southern Watch' and 'Enduring Freedom'.

Above: The Persian Gulf 2003: an F-14D Super Tomcat assigned to the 'Bounty Hunters' of Fighter Squadron Two (VF-2) aboard the USS *Constellation* (CV 64) has been prepared for another mission and loaded with four 1,000lb GBU-16 Laser-Guided Bombs (LGBs) in support of Operation 'Iraqi Freedom'. Initially, the Tomcat could carry only conventional 'dumb' bombs, and had no precision guided munition capability. However, the ability to deliver laser-guided bombs such as the GBU-10, GBU-12, GBU-16 and GBU-24 was added in 1994, even though the Tomcat initially had to rely on other aircraft to laser-designate the targets.

Right: An F-14B Tomcat strike fighter assigned to Fighter Squadron One Zero Two (VF-102) on board the aircraft carrier USS *George Washington* (CVN 73) in the Persian Gulf, December 2, 1997. *George Washington* and VF-102 were conducting Operation 'Southern Watch' in the Persian Gulf in support of UN sanctions against Iraq. The aircraft is armed with 500lb Mk 82 'dumb' bombs as well as Phoenix and Sidewinder air-to-air missiles.

Above: A 482nd Fighter Wing (93rd Fighter Squadron) F-16C Fighting Falcon near the southern Florida coastline over Homestead Air Reserve Base. The aircraft carries a single GBU-12 laser guided bomb, AIM-120 and AIM-9 air-to-air missiles, ALQ-131 jamming pod, a LANTIRN targeting pod and a 370-US gallon external fuel tank. The F-16 was originally conceived as a lightweight air combat plane but has matured into a sophisticated multi-role war plane well able to fulfil the attack profile.

Below: During Operation 'Iraqi Freedom', an F-16 Fighting Falcon assigned to the 157th Expeditionary Fighter Squadron prepares to take off on a combat sortie from a forward-deployed location. Under the starboard wing can be seen a 370-US gallon external fuel tank, a 2,000lb Mk 84 JDAM GPS guided bomb, an AIM-120 AMRAAM air-to-air missile and, under the fuselage, a LANTIRN pod.

Above: An F-16C/J Falcon from the 52nd Fighter Wing based at Spandahlem AB, Germany moves in to receive fuel from a KC-135R Stratotanker with the 100th Air Expeditionary Wing from RAF Mildenhall, UK, on March 31, 1999, while patrolling the skies over Kosovo during Operation 'Allied Force'. It is armed with AIM-120C AMRAAM missiles for self protection and Highspeed Anti Radiation Missiles (HARM) on the inboard stations to suppress anti-aircraft radar sites.

Below: An F-16 Fighting Falcon fires a HARM missile against an Iraqi radar site that had locked on to coalition aircraft which were enforcing the Southern No-Fly Zone. The F-16 has a maximum speed of 1,320mph, a service ceiling of over 50,000ft, and a combat radius of 340 miles on a hi-lo-hi mission profile with 6,000lb of bombs/missiles.

Opposite page, top and bottom: Ground crew check Mk 84 2,000lb bombs as the ordnance is readied for loading aboard 401st Tactical Fighter Wing F-16 attack planes. These aircraft conducted some of the first daylight strikes against Iraqi targets during Operation 'Desert Storm'.

Above: An F-16 being readied for take-off for an attack on Iraq during Operation 'Desert Storm'. On each wing, as well as carrying 2,000lb Mk 84 'dumb' bombs, the plane is equipped with Sidewinder air-to-air missiles.

Right: In the skies over Afghanistan in March 2002, a US Navy F/A-18 Hornet assigned to the 'Knighthawks' of Strike Fighter Squadron One Three Six (VFA-136) conducts a patrol mission during Operation 'Enduring Freedom'. The plane is armed with one Mk 82 JDAM bomb on its port wing and two 500lb GBU-12 laser guided bombs on the starboard wing. Under the fuselage can be seen the Forward Looking Infra-Red (FLIR) pod as well as the large external fuel tank.

Above: On a bombing mission, an F/A-18 Hornet is ready for aerial refueling with a KC-135R from the 319th Air Expeditionary Group. The 319th AEG was deployed to a forward location in support of Operation 'Enduring Freedom' over Afghanistan. The Hornet is armed with at least two GBU-12 500lb laser-guided bombs, plus two Sidewinder missiles.

Below: November 4, 2001: an F/A-18 Hornet from the carrier USS *Carl Vinson* of the 'Mighty Shrikes' of Strike Fighter Squadron Nine Four (VFA-94), carries a strike payload consisting of an AIM-9 Sidewinder missile and 2,000lb Mk 84 JDAM (Joint Direct Attack Munition) GPS-guided bombs in support of Operation 'Enduring Freedom'.

Above: At sea aboard USS *John C. Stennis* (CVN 74) March 8, 2002. Aviation ordnancemen from the 'Argonauts' of Strike Fighter Squadron One Four Seven (VFA-147) load a 1,000lb GBU-31, Joint Direct Attack Munition (JDAM) onto an F/A-18 Hornet Strike Fighter in support of Operation 'Enduring Freedom'.

Right: Aboard the aircraft carrier USS *Theodore Roosevelt*, in April 1999, aviation ordnancemen load Rockeye cluster bombs onto the wing of an F/A-18 Hornet. At the time the USS *Theodore Roosevelt* (CVN 71) was deployed to the Adriatic Sea in support of the NATO Operation 'Allied Force' to liberate Kosovo.

Above and left: Aviation ordnancemen move and attach Mk 83 1,000lb 'dumb' bombs to an F/A-18E Super Hornet on the flight deck aboard USS *Abraham Lincoln* (CVN 72). *Lincoln* and Carrier Air Wing Fourteen (CVW-14) were deployed to the Persian Gulf in support of Operation 'Iraqi Freedom'. The fins attached to these Mk 83 general purpose bombs are the BSU-85/B Air-Inflatable Retarder (AIR), designed for dropping at low altitude. The fin deploys high drag inflated 'ballutes' (balloon/parachutes) after release in order to affect the trajectory and speed of the falling bomb so it will avoid exploding underneath the plane dropping it. Even though modern war is very 'hi-tec', there are still demands for old-fashioned muscle power on a carrier's flight deck as these ordnancemen lift a 1,000lb bomb onto the aircraft's wing pylon.

Above: An F/A-18 Hornet from Strike Fighter Squadron One Three One (VFA-131) flies equipped with a 1,000lb GBU-31 Joint Direct Attack Munition (JDAM) mounted under its starboard (right) wing. On the port wing is a 1,000lb GBU-16 laser-guided bomb. VFA-131 is part of Carrier Air Wing Seven (CVW-7), deployed aboard USS *John F. Kennedy,* and was conducting combat missions in support of Operation 'Enduring Freedom'.

Right: Aviation ordnancemen of Strike Fighter Squadron Eight Seven (VFA-87) stand in front of the ship's island with pallets of 1,000lb Mk 83 'dumb' bombs. All Mk 80 series general purpose bombs aboard ships are required to be thermally protected as indicated by the rough and bumpy exterior surface of these weapons.

Left: Two F/A-18Cs from VFA-82. The aircraft in the foreground is carrying two drill rounds of the AGM-84 Harpoon anti-ship missile on the wing pylons. The Harpoon entered service in 1977 and is in service with the US Navy and Air Force. The sea-skimming missile has a warhead weighing 490lbs and a range of 60 miles. It was succesfully used in the Gulf of Sirte against Libyan warships.

Left: The AGM-84 Harpoon served as the basis for the modified AGM-84E Stand-off Land Attack Missile (SLAM). This involved replacing the Harpoon's seeker head with an Imaging Infra-Red (IIR) seeker from the AGM-65D Maverick plus a GPS receiver and a datalink. SLAM entered service in 1990 and was used very successfully against land targets during Operation 'Desert Storm'.

Left: The Standoff Land Attack Missile Expanded Response (SLAM-ER), an evolutionary upgrade to the combat-proven SLAM day/night, adverse-weather over-the-horizon, precision strike missile. The SLAM-ER is shorter and is used exclusively by US Navy F/A-18 squadrons.

Right: Aboard the USS *Abraham Lincoln* an F/A-18C Hornet assigned to the 'Fist of the Fleet' Strike Fighter Squadron Two Five (VFA-25) sits ready on the portside number four catapult. This particular Hornet is outfitted with a number of strike weapons including the Standoff Land Attack Missile Expanded Response (SLAM-ER) located on the aircraft's starboard wing pylon. *Abraham Lincoln* and her embarked Carrier Air Wing Fourteen (CVW-14) were conducting combat missions in support of Operations 'Enduring Freedom' and 'Southern Watch'.

Below: The AGM-88 High-Speed Anti-Radiation Missile (HARM) is an air-to-surface tactical missile designed to seek out and destroy enemy radar-equipped defense systems. The guidance system homes in on enemy radar emissions. The HARM was approved for full production in 1983. It is operationally deployed by the US Air Force, Marines, and Navy. The missile proved very effective against Libyan targets in the Gulf of Sirte in 1986 and in the conflicts with Iraq and Serbia.

Above: US Marines load AGM-88A HARM missiles under the wings of an F/A-18 attack plane of the Marine Corps Fighter/Attack Squadron Four Five One (VMFA-451) during Operation 'Desert Storm' in 1991. The fins to the missiles are attached after loading onto the aircraft.

Below: A US Navy F/A-18 Hornet armed with a HARM ground attack anti-radar missile and two AMRAAM air-to-air missiles on a mission in support of Operation 'Iraqi Freedom'. The Hornet is primarily used as a fighter escort and for fleet air defense. However, it is also a very fine attack aircraft with the capability of force projection and interdiction, as well as both close and deep air support. This duel capability gives commanders immense flexibility in wartime operations.

Above: Over the Middle East, an F/A-18 Hornet assigned to the aircraft carrier USS *Harry S. Truman*, conducts refuelling operations with a US Air Force KC-135R Stratotanker. The aircraft has a GBU-12 LGB under its starboard wing and a 1,000lb JDAM under its port wing, plus a couple of Sidewinder missiles.

Below: The USS *Harry S. Truman* and Carrier Air Wing Three (CVW-3) were deployed for combat missions in support of Operation 'Iraqi Freedom'. In the hangar bay aboard *Truman* (CVN 75), a sailor assigned to the 'Gunslingers' Strike Fighter Squadron One Zero Five (VFA-105), prepares to paint on the side of an F/A-18 Hornet the mission tally that it has completed during the course of the operation.

Above: US Marine Corps AV-8B Harrier II attack planes from Marine Attack Squadron Five One Three (VMA-513) fly in formation during Operation 'Desert Shield' in 1990. The Marine Corps are the only US operators of this unique warplane, with its short take-off and vertical landing capabilities (STOVL). The first Harriers were designed and flew in Great Britain in the 1960s. The aircraft has been updated and extensively improved and the AV-8B is a larger, longer-range, and generally more powerful aircraft than the earlier models.

Below: Flight deck crewmen aboard the amphibious assault ship USS *Nassau* (LHA) refuel two Marine Corps AV-8B Harriers as a third makes a vertical landing during Operation 'Desert Shield'.

Above and below: The earlier generation Harrier, the AV-8A, had reached its operational limit and was replaced by the larger and more potent AV-8B beginning in 1984. The AV-8B Harrier II was to see its first combat during Operation 'Desert Storm' in 1991 and as a result of this experience improvements were made. During 'Desert Storm' the Harrier II performed very well, even though five aircraft were lost to enemy action. In these pre-upgrade pictures, in the lower photograph note the Glazed Nose Aperture (GNA) of the Hughes Angle Rate Bombing Set (ARBS) and, just behind it, the Forward Looking Infra-Red (FLIR) sensor denoted by the bump just in front of the cockpit. The FLIR is an extremely useful device in detecting and designating targets.

US Marine Corps AV-8B Harrier II attack aircraft from Marine Attack Squadron Five One Three (VMA-513) during 'Desert Shield'. The weapons that the AV-8B can carry can include Mk 82/83 dumb bombs, rocket pods, cluster bombs, GBU-12/16 laser-guided bombs, Maverick air-to-ground guided missiles, Sidewinder and AMRAAM air-to-air missiles and a five-barrelled 25mm GAU-12 cannon.

Above: At sea aboard the amphibious ship USS *Peleliu* (LHA 5) in support of Operation 'Enduring Freedom', a US Marine Corps pilot assigned to the 15th Marine Expeditionary Unit carefully inspects his AV-8B Harrier prior to a mission over Afghanistan. Attached to the wing pylons are Mk 83 1,000lb general purpose bombs. Because of the increased risk of fire on warships while in combat situations, bombs aboard US warships require thermal protection, as indicated by the rough and bumpy exterior surface of these weapons.

.

Below: Also on USS *Peleliu,* an aircraft technician with the 15th Marine Expeditionary Unit scrawls a message to the terrorists on the surface of a 500lb Mk 82 bomb. Marine pilots bombed Taliban targets during Harrier airstrikes as part of Operation 'Enduring Freedom'.

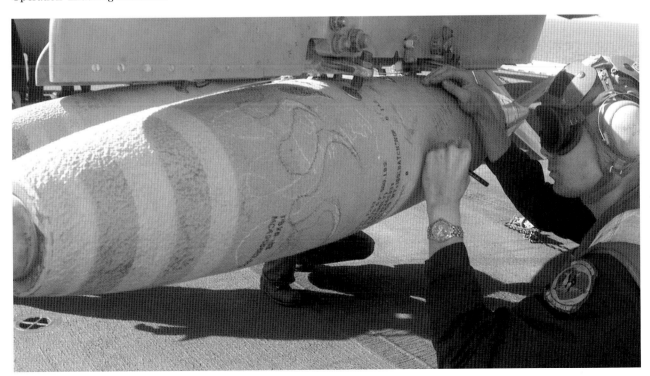

At sea aboard USS *Nassau,* US Marine AV-8B Harrier vertical and/or short take-off and landing (V/STOL) strike aircraft stand parked at the aft end of the amphibious assault ship's flight deck. The AV-8B is an all-rounder, capable of attacking and destroying both surface and air targets, reconnaissance tasks and conducting other air operations, such as escorting helicopters. These are Harrier II Plus which incorporate many improvements over the earlier models, particularly with the installation of the APG-65 radar, as denoted by the slightly more bulbous nose in which the antenna is housed.

Above: An AV-8B Harrier Plus from the 24th Marine Expeditionary Unit (24th MEU) Air Combat Element (ACE) commences its 'roll take off' outward-bound from the amphibious assault ship USS *Nassau* (LHA 4) to engage targets over Iraq in support of Operation 'Iraqi Freedom'. The inboard pylon of the plane's port wing carries a GBU-12 laser-guided bomb and on the starboard inboard pylon a laser pod for targeting. On the outer pylons are two external fuel tanks.

Right: Aviation ordnancemen inspect a GBU-16 1,000lb bomb for its correct configuration and any visible defects. Controllable canards have yet to be attached before assembly is complete, two of which are lying on the tail unit of the weapon.

Left: Aviation ordnancemen assigned to the 'Top Hatters' of Strike Fighter Squadron One Four (VFA-14) load GBU-12 laser-guided munitions onto an F/A-18E Super Hornet on the flight deck aboard USS *Nimitz* (CVN 68). *Nimitz* and Carrier Air Wing Eleven (CVW-11) were deployed in support of Operation 'Iraqi Freedom'.

Left: An aviation ordnanceman gathers the guided bomb unit (GBU) laser-guided seeker head covers from an F/A-18C Hornet aboard USS *Abraham Lincoln* (CVN 72) which was conducting combat operations in support of Operation 'Iraqi Freedom'.

Above and below: The GBU-15 is an unpowered glide weapon used to destroy high-value enemy targets. This highly maneuverable weapon has a low-to-medium altitude delivery capability with pinpoint accuracy. The GBU-15, with television guidance, completed full-scale operational tests and evaluation in 1983 and, in 1985, tests with an imaging infrared guidance seeker. It also has a standoff capability. During Operation 'Desert Storm' F-111F pilots used GBU-15 glide bombs to successfully seal the oil pipeline manifolds sabotaged by Saddam Hussein's troops.

Above: A GBU-15 being test-dropped from a F-4 Phantom. The GBU-15 is generally a 2,000lb Mk 82 GP bomb with tail and nose sections strapped on to it. There is also the BLU-109/B hardened penetrator bomb and the system has been evaluated with a cluster munition canister. GBU-15s were used with great effect during Operation 'Desert Storm' in 1991. The mighty Phantom saw service for over 30 years with the USAF, USN and USMC and was the most important US Fighter/Attack plane in service during the postwar period. First seeing combat in Vietnam during the mid 1960s it went on to see victory with Operation 'Desert Storm' in 1991. Retired from US service in the early 1990s, it is still in service with at least half a dozen countries worldwide.

Below: US Air Force weapons personnel prepare an F-15 Strike Eagle in support of NATO Operation 'Allied Force'. The aircraft is being armed with Sidewinder air-to-air missiles and at least one AGM-130, which is basically a GBU-15 glide bomb with a rocket motor attached to its underside giving it a greatly increased potential for penetrating targets.

Above: Service members from the 379th EMXX (AMMO) Squadron roll out an AGM-130 rocket-powered bomb to deliver to the flight line at this forward-deployed location on March 21, 2003. The 379th Ammo squadron assembled more than 5,000 bombs in four weeks for aircraft use in support of Operation 'Enduring Freedom'.

Below: Bomb loaders from the 335th Expeditionary Fighter Squadron prepare to mount an AGM-130 rocket powered bomb to an F-15E Strike Eagle for a mission at a forward-deployed location on March 21, 2003. The Strike Eagles are deployed in support of military operations in the Middle East.

Left: F/A-18C Hornets fly in formation over the desert during Operation 'Desert Storm'. The foremost of the aircraft is armed with Mk 20 Rockeye cluster bombs as well as Sidewinder and Sparrow missiles. The next Hornet along has HARM missiles mounted under the wing stations.

Below: Aviation ordnancemen transport Mk 20 Rockeye II cluster bombs across the flight deck of the aircraft carrier USS *Saratoga* (CV 60).

Opposite page, top: Maintenance crewmen from Attack Squadron Thirty Four (VA-34) move a weapons skid loaded with Mk 20 Rockeye II cluster bombs across the flight deck of the nuclear-powered aircraft carrier USS *Dwight D. Eisenhower* (CVN 69). The *Eisenhower* was on station in the Persian Gulf in response to Iraq's invasion of Kuwait in 1991.

Opposite page, bottom: The 500lb GBU-22, foreground, and the 2,000lb GBU-24 Paveway III low-level laser-guided bombs.

Above left: A ground crewman readies a 332nd Air Expeditionary Group active duty F-15E Strike Eagle. On the wing of the Eagle is a GBU-15 2,000lb glide bomb and above it is an AIM-9 Sidewinder.

Above: A 332nd Air Expeditionary Group F-15E Eagle has a GBU-24 2,000lb bomb slung under the aircraft's fuselage and, on the wing pylon, an AIM-9 Sidewinder air-to-air missile along with a 370-US gallon external fuel tank.

Left and opposite page, top and bottom: USAF technicians loading an AGM-154A Joint Stand-Off Weapon (JSOW) onto an attack plane. The JSOW is an adverse-weather, short-range, stand-off anti-armor/SEAD (Suppression of Enemy Air Defenses) dispenser weapon. It is designed to deliver sub-munitions in much the same way as a cluster bomb does. The wings, seen here folded back, aid the weapon during the glide stage of an attack. It was first used during Operation 'Allied Force' in 1999, USN F/A-18s using it to attack Serbian SAM radars. Targeting is achieved in the same manner as the JDAM.

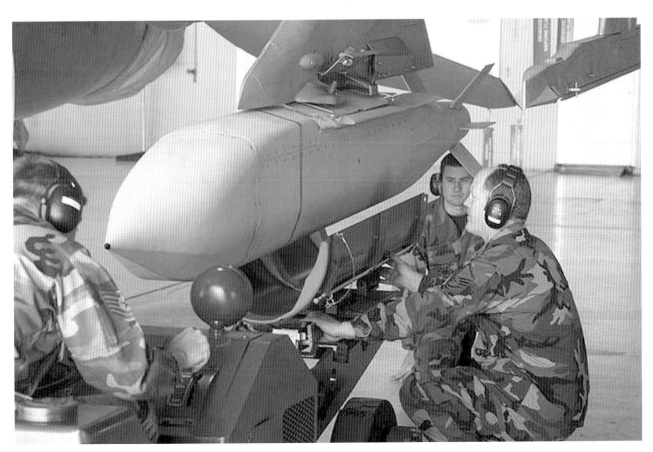

Above and left: The A-10 Thunderbolt II is built to survive direct hits from anti-aircraft guns as large as 23mm caliber. These views are of the tail section of a 23rd Tactical Fighter Wing A-10A attack plane that had sustained damage when a Russian-built SA-16 anti-aircraft missile detonated very close by during Operation 'Desert Storm'.

Right: 'Bridge Busting'. A bridge over the Euphrates River cut by attack planes during 'Desert Storm'.

Below: 'Tank Plinking'. A destroyed Iraqi T-55 main battle tank lies amidst other destroyed vehicles along the highway between Kuwait City and Basra – 'The Highway of Death' – following the retreat of Iraqi forces from Kuwait during Operation 'Desert Storm'. 'Like shooting fish in a barrel' was the way one pilot was quoted when describing the attack.

Opposite page, top and centre: Views of Iraqi hardened aircraft shelters at Al-Salman Air Base after they had taken direct hits by precision guided weapons during 'Desert Storm'.

Opposite page, bottom: A munitions bunker at Al-Salman Air Base destroyed by Coalition attack planes during 'Desert Storm'.

Above: A large bridge that has been destroyed by the Coalition precision bombing attacks during 'Desert Storm'.

Right: A wrecked Iraqi radar dish shredded during the Coalition aerial onslaught of 1991.

Above: The EA-6B Prowler is the only tactical electronic warfare jammer aircraft currently in service with the US. The aircraft airframe is based on the retired A-6 Intruder. The Prowler has an attack capability to augment its electronic offensive abilities, with the use of HARMs. This capabilty has been put to good use to-date during the many combats with Iraq since 'Desert Storm' in 1991, and against Serbia in 1999.

Opposite page, top: Though not now in service, the A-6E Intruder saw war service in Vietnam, the attacks on Libya and Lebanon. The A-6 also made retaliatory attacks on Iranian warships in the 1980s and took part in Operation 'Desert Storm', where it saw its last combat missions. The A-6 could carry a huge weapon load of 18,000lbs and could accommodate just about every piece of ordnance in the Navy's and Marines' inventories.

Below: A-7E Corsair of Attack Squadron Seven Two (VA-72) heading for a target in Iraq during 'Desert Storm'. The Corsair is also no longer in US service. With a long and proud history, the A-7 saw war service in Vietnam, the attacks on Libya, Lebanon, and Grenada. The A-7 also made retaliatory attacks on Iranian oil platforms and Iranian warships, as well as serving in 'Desert Storm'. The aircraft below is armed with eight Mk 82 500lb retarded bombs for use at low level. A Sidewinder missile can also be seen on the side of the fuselage.

Opposite page, bottom: A Corsair dropping two retarded bombs. The MAU-91A/B fin assembly on the bombs is a retarded fin that consists of four folding drag plates which open shortly after the bomb is released, slowing the flight of the bomb and distancing it from the plane.

Above and below: The F-111 is also not now in service. It saw war service in Vietnam, the attacks on Libya and during 'Desert Storm'. During its day the swing-wing F-111 proved itself to be world's premier pinpoint attack plane. It was retired from US service in 1998. The picture above is an F-111F of the 494th Tactical Fighter Squadron of the 48th Tactical Fighter Wing about to take off for a mission during 'Desert Storm'. It is armed with laser-guided bombs.